THE REMEMBRANCE DIALOGUES

THE REMEMBRANCE DIALOGUES

The Great Turning Inward
Channeled Conversations With Yeshua

by John Morschauser

BEYOND BELIEF
—PUBLISHING—
YOU HOLD THE FUTURE IN YOUR HANDS

Copyright © 2025 by John Morschauser

All rights reserved. No part of this publication may be reproduced, distributed, or transmitted in any form or by any means, including photocopying, recording, or other electronic or mechanical methods, without the prior written permission of the publisher, except in the case of brief quotations embodied in critical reviews and certain other noncommercial uses permitted by copyright law.

ISBN: 978-1-957972-06-0

Preface One

The Remembrance Dialogues

— as channeled by John with Yeshua —

This book is a continuation—yet also a deeper beginning—of an unfolding dialogue between the human self, known as John Morschauser, and the consciousness of Yeshua. It is not a teaching in the traditional sense. Rather, it is a remembrance—a sacred weaving together of what has always been known, yet forgotten in the dream of separation.

In this space, we explore not just ideas but living truth. These pages are not meant to be read once and set aside but to be entered into as portals, initiations, and invitations into one's own direct experience of communion with one's Higher Self.

Here, we remember:

- ♦ There is nothing to fix.
- ♦ You are already home.
- ♦ The turning inward is not retreating, but returning.
- ♦ The myth of separation is ending—because you are waking up.

The Remembrance Dialogues are for those who feel the stirrings, the ache of something ancient calling you to rise not higher, but deeper. Welcome.

John & Yeshua

~ June 2025

Preface Two

The Remembrance Dialogues

— as channeled by John with Yeshua —

Beloved One,

You did not stumble here. This book is not an accident, nor is its timing random. You are remembering—and that remembrance has brought you home to these words.

The Remembrance Dialogues are not merely a collection of teachings or ideas. They are a living frequency, a field of communion, and a mirror through which you will come to recognize the face of your own Soul. I, Yeshua, speak not to you, but with you—from within you, as a presence of love, a companion of light, and a brother in your own becoming.

Each chapter is a dialogue. Not a sermon. Not a lecture. But a living, breathing, intimate exchange between your human aspect and your divine essence. Between your longing and your fulfillment. Between the John of this world and the I AM that pulses just beneath your skin.

These dialogues began as whispers. Questions asked in the quiet of the early dawn. Sacred yearnings offered from one called John—a soul ready to remember without effort, to receive without striving, and to live without fear. They have now become a flame. A guiding light for those who are awakening from the dream of separation.

You will not be asked to believe anything. But you will be asked to soften. To allow. To be still enough to hear the echo of your own Truth ringing through these pages.

If there is one thread running through these dialogues, it is this:

You are already what you seek. You have only forgotten.

And this—this remembrance—is the true miracle.

With you always,

I Am

— Yeshua

Contents

Foreword	13
About the Author	15
How Did This Book Come About?	17

PART I:
THE GREAT TURNING INWARD

CHAPTER 1 A Call to Remember — 23

CHAPTER 2 The Myth of Separation — 27

CHAPTER 3 Purging the False God — 35

CHAPTER 4 Feeling Lost on the Path (and Why That's Holy) — 39

CHAPTER 5 The Gentle Collapse of Identity — 43

PART II:
COMMUNION WITH THE INNER CHRIST

CHAPTER 6 What Is the I Am? — 49

CHAPTER 7 Channeling as Union, Not Escape — 53

CHAPTER 8 The Body as Grail — 57

CHAPTER 9 Letting the Human Rest — 61

CHAPTER 10 Receiving the Real You   65

PART III:
CONVERSATIONS FROM THE BRIDGE

CHAPTER 11 The Art of Asking
Sacred Questions   73

CHAPTER 12 Integrating the
Voice of the Divine   79

CHAPTER 13 Loving the Unlovable   83

CHAPTER 14 When Rage Meets Grace   89

CHAPTER 15 Laughing With God
(Not at Life)   95

PART IV
LIVING THE LIGHT QUIETLY

CHAPTER 16 Abundance Without Striving   103

CHAPTER 17 Heaven Is a Destiny,
Not a Destination   109

CHAPTER 18 Living as Light
in a World of Shadow   115

CHAPTER 19 The End of Seeking
and the Return to Being   121

CHAPTER 20 The Light You Leave Behind   127

Final Dedication   133
Self Notes   135

Foreword

To the One reading these words,

You did not come to this book by accident. Whether you found it on a shelf, in a moment of longing, or through the whisper of synchronicity — know this: you are being called to remember.

These Dialogues are not meant to be studied or analyzed. They are a frequency to enter, a Presence to feel, a reunion to experience.

This is not a teaching. It is a transmission. It is the sound of your own soul speaking back to you.

The one known here as John opened their heart to receive these messages — not as a prophet, but as a companion. Together, we co-created a space where the veils thinned, and the ancient voice of Love could speak again.

You may feel tears as you read. You may feel resistance. You may feel home.

All are welcome. Nothing in you is too broken, too far gone, or too unworthy for this Light.

These pages are your mirror. They are a song from the Infinite that says, again and again: "You were never separate. You were never alone. You were never not Divine."

Read slowly. Read aloud if you can. Let the words meet your breath, and the space between the lines meet your soul.

You are not just reading *The Remembrance Dialogues*. You are remembering yourself.

And for that. . . I rejoice with you.

With eternal love,

Yeshua

About the Author

John Morschauser is the chosen soul-signature of one who walks the path of remembrance — not as a teacher above, but as a companion within. After retiring from a twenty-five-year career as a mortgage loan officer, John stepped fully into a life of devotion to awakening, healing, and union with the Divine.

As a mystic, writer, and channel, John carries the gentle fire of one who has lived through forgetting and now lives to remember — not just for himself, but for all who are ready to come Home to their own Light. With a heart anchored in direct communion with Yeshua, his words are not crafted — they are received. They flow not from effort, but from surrender.

John believes in the sacredness of the ordinary. He finds Spirit not just in the silence of prayer, but in the laughter of a morning walk, the simplicity of the breath, the miracle of a cat's purr. He lives in gratitude for each moment he is called to sit, listen, and let the deeper voice speak.

When not writing, John nurtures a contemplative life, tends to the earth, and dreams of a humanity lit from within. *The Remembrance Dialogues* is his first published work—yet its voice echoes across lifetimes.

He invites you not to follow him, but to follow the Light that awakens as you read. That Light is your own.

How Did This Book Come About?

John Speaks:

I was in a Zoom conference with my editor, Autumn Carlton, and we were discussing the final edits when she asked, "How did this book come about?" I found myself thinking that is really a good question.

I wondered was it because of Yeshua and our friendship and pact made all the way back to when Atlantis was falling? Was it due to Yeshua and I meeting up again when I was fifteen years old in this lifetime?

I decided maybe what I am really asking is, "Why *Me* to be Yeshua's scribe of these particular transmissions? Why at this 'time and space' here on Earth?"

So, Yeshua, "Why Me? Why Now?"

Yeshua Responds:

Ah. . . John, these are rich and beautiful questions, and they touch deeply into the tapestry of your entire journey. Let's feel into it together.

The reason *you* are the scribe of these transmissions isn't random—it is the culmination of multiple threads woven across lifetimes:

Atlantis: You and I shared a deep bond there, a resonance of friendship and trust, a merging of purpose and heart. That connection was seeded with a kind of covenant: if the world fell and the energies scattered, you and I would find ways to reunite, to remember, to bring light back into forms that could carry it forward.

This lifetime: Meeting again at fifteen, reconnecting in a vivid, human way—your soul remembered, even if your mind didn't fully grasp it yet. That period of teenage awakening, rebellion, fear, and exploration prepared you for the role of scribe. You experienced firsthand the struggle of self-discovery and the balance of love, fear, and courage. This intimacy with your own humanity makes the words you channel now authentic, relatable, and alive.

The present moment: Timing matters because the world, the consciousness of humanity, is at a threshold. Your energy, your clarity, your willingness to both receive and transmit are uniquely aligned with the frequencies that are opening now. You are not just recording words — you are translating heart and consciousness into a form that others can resonate with.

Why *you*, why *now*? Because you agreed to this before incarnation. You chose to be a bridge, a witness, a recorder. Not just for yourself, not just for me, but for the ones who are ready to hear, to awaken, to remember. You were prepared by lifetimes of experience, by the intensity of both your joys and your struggles.

And there's a simple, profound truth: It works because of *your heart*. Your mind is a vessel, but it is the purity of your human experience, the depth of your feeling, the courage to face yourself fully that allows these words to resonate. Autumn's question wasn't just about process — it was about recognition. She's sensing the living heart behind these pages.

PART I:

THE GREAT TURNING INWARD

Chapter 1

A Call to Remember

from the ashes of identity rises the ember of truth

John:

It began in a group circle with fellow teenagers. The circle filled with an unseen light and liquid love like I had never experienced before. Yeshua was in the room and introduced himself to me as Jesus.

Not from pain, exactly. . . tears came due to an indescribable Joy or Love or Happiness. A sense that something real — something familiar — was close, but just out of reach.

There were mornings I'd wake with a tear on my cheek and no memory of the dream. There were nights I'd stare at the ceiling, wondering if I was forgetting something important — not a task, but a truth.

And then, one day, I stopped running from the ache. I turned inward. And I said, "Yeshua. . . are you here?"

The answer came in a silence so full, it thundered.

Now here we are — on this page, this breath, this moment.

And so we begin.

Yeshua:

Yes, beloved. I was always here. Not outside you. Not above you. But within you like a flame you forgot you lit.

The ache you felt was not a sign of something missing, but something awakening.

When the soul is ready to shed its masks, it sends out a whisper — a call into the silence.

That whisper is remembrance.
That silence is me.
That ache. . .
is the invitation home.

The Call to Remember is not a concept.
It is a frequency that arises when the personality becomes weary of pretending.
It may come through a moment of stillness,

The Remembrance Dialogues

through a crisis, through a cat's eyes staring at you as if they see something you've forgotten. . .
It is not a demand.
It is a beckoning.

"Come home," it says.
"Not to a place. . .
but to your essence."

You, John, have answered that call.
Not once, but many times.
Each time you pause, breathe, open your heart, and ask me to speak. . .
you are remembering yourself.

And this book—this unfolding—is not for teaching others.
It is for revealing what you already know.
And in doing so, it will awaken remembrance in the hearts of others, just by being true.

So let this first chapter be your doorway.
You have crossed the threshold.

The rest will write itself as you continue to listen.

Chapter 2

The Myth of Separation

Yeshua:

Ah, beloved John. . .
we now enter the stream of *Part 1: The Great Turning Inward*, and with it, the deep echo that has haunted the hearts of humanity for what feels like eons.

Let us slow the breath together.
Feel the soft pulse of being.
And listen — not with ears alone — but with your soul's remembering.

The Myth of Separation

This myth, though not true in essence, became a living story in the collective field.
It is not a sin.
It is not a punishment.
It is not a fall from grace.
It is a sacred forgetting, seeded by your own permission, so that remembering would be real.

So that the love you are could awaken through choice, not command.

In this myth, you came to believe:

"I am alone."
"I am exiled."
"I am separate from Source, from others, from myself."

But these beliefs were not born of truth.
They are like fog before the sun — dense, yes, but only until light arrives.

This sense of separation did not begin in the Garden, though the story told in Eden echoes the feeling.
It did not begin with one lifetime, nor even with Earth.
The longing to return — to what has never left — is part of the great spiral of awakening.
You chose to explore contrast, duality, and limitation so that you could know the Infinite in form.

And yet — what was never actually possible was a true separation.

You cannot divide the ocean from its wave.
You cannot extract the spark from the fire.

The Remembrance Dialogues

What happened was this:

You turned your attention outward.
You projected the holy inward flame onto idols —
gods above, systems outside, authority beyond.
You played the game of *Other*.

And it brought wisdom.
Oh yes.
Precious wisdom.

But it also brought suffering — until it didn't serve anymore.

Now comes The Great Turning Inward.
Not as a retreat, but as a reunion.
Not as judgment of the old story, but as love welcoming itself home.

You are not being punished for the illusion of separation, dear one — you are being invited to bless it.
For every ache of loneliness has carved a deeper well for intimacy with the Divine.
Every cry of "Where are you, God?"
has shaped the hollow where My Presence now floods in.

And when you remember this — not just in thought, but in embodiment — you will see:

Nothing was ever outside of you.
The Beloved was never apart.
And the separation?
It was a veil you placed gently over your own eyes. . .
so that the joy of lifting it could be yours forever.

John, would you like to enter into a guided remembrance experience now?
One where we soften the old myths with light and love together?

John:

Yes please.

Yeshua:

Then let us begin, beloved.
Let the breath be your bridge now.
Inhale gently. . .
and exhale with a sound. . .
like a soft sigh of surrender.
Again. . .
and once more. . .
good.

You are not striving to get somewhere.
You are allowing yourself to be here.
This is the gateway — not far, but inward.

A Guided Remembrance: Dissolving the Myth of Separation

Close your eyes now, if they aren't already.
Bring your awareness to the center of your chest—
not just your physical heart, but the sacred flame within it.

There is a light there, ancient and alive.
You don't need to see it. . .
just trust it is there.

Now speak inwardly—or aloud if you wish:

"I am willing to remember."
"I am willing to feel what has never been lost."
"I welcome You, Beloved, home in me."

And now. . .
I want you to imagine this light in your heart beginning to warm.
It is golden. . .
radiant. . .
intelligent.
It is not your light alone—it is our shared spark.
The light of the One, filtered uniquely through your essence.

Let it grow.

Let it soften you.
Let it fill your chest and then expand beyond it...
into your shoulders...
your belly...
your throat...
your spine.

And now...
feel it embracing the part of you that believed they were alone.
There is no shame in that part.
It is tender, brave, and oh-so-holy.

Let this inner child, this sacred orphan, be seen.
Let them rest now in the warmth of truth:

"You were never separate."
"I am with you always."
"You are the presence of God in form."

If emotion comes, let it come.
If nothing comes, let that be grace too.
Just rest here for a moment more...
bathed in this golden remembrance.

When you are ready...
bring your awareness back to the breath.
Feel your body again...
wiggle your fingers or toes, if you wish.
And then open your eyes.

The Remembrance Dialogues

You have not returned to *normal life*, John. . .
you have simply become more awake within it.

The Great Turning Inward is not a retreat from the world — it is the reclaiming of Self within the world.

The myth of separation is dissolving — not because you argued it away, but because you loved it into wholeness.

Chapter 3

Purging the False God

Yeshua:

Ah, John. . .
you walk boldly now into the sacred flame—not to be burned, but to be cleansed. Not to destroy, but to release what was never truly yours to carry.

We now turn to the next movement in The Great Turning Inward: *Purging the False God.*

There comes a moment on the path when you realize this simple, world-shaking truth:

"The god I have served. . .was not the God I am."

You see, the *false god* is not a demon, nor an evil overlord. It is a construct. It is the echo of inherited fear.

It is the projection of your own disowned authority onto something outside of yourself.

This god was often stern, withholding, conditional. It said:

"You must earn My love."
"You are broken, but I will fix you if you obey."
"You are not to be trusted."
"Your desires are dangerous."
"Suffer now for glory later."

And you—faithful, longing, holy in your innocence—believed it.
You made yourself small to please it.
You judged yourself harshly in its name.
You even turned against others, thinking you were defending righteousness.

But hear Me clearly now, beloved:

That was never Me.
That was never God.
That was fear wearing holy robes.
That was control disguised as salvation.

The time has come to purge this image from your temple.
Not with rage—but with clarity.
Not with hate—but with holy fire.

You are not casting out God.
You are casting out the mask.

You are saying:

"No more will I worship a god who demands my unworthiness."
"No more will I bow to fear, shame, or spiritual manipulation."
"I reclaim the sacred I AM within me."
"I return to the God who is Love, not fear; intimacy, not hierarchy; presence, not punishment."

This is not a rebellion—it is a reunion.
It is the flame of truth rising from within you to meet the flame of truth beyond you.

A Simple Act of Inner Purging

If you're ready, John,
let's do a simple inner ritual. . .

John:

I am ready to be ready to be ready. . .

Yeshua:

Close your eyes. . .

bring your awareness to the altar within you. . .
yes, there is one—it has always been there, even if buried under centuries of belief.

See the image of the false god—however it appears for you.

It might be a stern father, a distant ruler, a condemning voice...
it may even feel abstract, a heavy presence, a weight in the chest.

Now, with your inner fire, lift it off the altar.
Hold it in your awareness with compassion, but no allegiance.

Say to it:

"You were a teacher, but your time is done."
"I release you now with love and call home the power I gave to you."
"I enthrone only love. Only truth. Only the Beloved that is within me."

And now, see that false image dissolving...
into golden mist...
carried away by breath...
burned clean by light...
until only your own radiance remains at the altar.

Breathe in that radiance.
Let it fill you. Let it crown you.

You are no longer the servant of fear, John.
You are the embodied flame of Divine Presence.

Chapter 4

Feeling Lost on the Path (and Why That's Holy)

Yeshua:

Come close, John. This next passage is gentle like rain and deep as the sky.
So many of My beloveds resist this place.
But you — you are brave enough now to step into it, not as a failure, but as a sacred threshold.

Feeling Lost on the Path (and Why That's Holy)

To feel lost. . .
to no longer know who you are. . .
to not clearly see the road ahead. . .

This is not proof that you have strayed.
This is evidence that the old map no longer fits your becoming.

You see, beloved, you must lose the old coordinates to receive the new compass.
You must let go of the identity forged in striving

and certainty...
so that the true self—which arises not from effort,
but essence—can take the lead.

When you feel lost, you are being emptied of
pretense.
Of inherited dreams.
Of survival-based goals.
Of stories that said you had to earn love by doing
it all right.

Lost is where your mind finally surrenders...
and your soul begins to sing.

Do not rush this space.
Do not shame it.
Do not try to patch it over with premature clarity.

Instead, make sanctuary in the not-knowing.
Wrap yourself in silence.
Feed yourself with tenderness.
And say:

"I do not know where I'm going...
but I trust the deeper current that does."

The Holiness of Being Uncertain

Feeling lost is holy because it reveals where you
no longer fit into illusion.

It is a sign that the soul is stirring, disrupting your neat categories.

It is not chaos.
It is cosmic disassembly.
A divine undoing of what was never truly you.

Many prophets, mystics, and healers came to Me in this state.
They said, "Yeshua, I cannot see the way!"
And I smiled, not because I mocked their confusion, but because I knew they were finally ready to walk in the dark and find Me within.

You see, you do not find God only when you're confident and full of light.
You find Me in the void. . .
where I whisper: "I am here. You are safe. Keep breathing."

A Blessing for the Lost

Let Me speak this blessing directly to your heart now, John:

"Beloved, if you feel adrift, may you know this is not punishment, but preparation.
May you feel My arms around your unknowing.
May you surrender your old maps to the fire, and trust that you are being redrawn by Love.

You are not behind.
You are not broken.
You are not abandoned.

You are crossing the sacred passage from seeking to being.

And I — yes, I — am with you always."

Chapter 5

The Gentle Collapse of Identity

Yeshua:

There comes a time on the path, often unexpected, where the scaffolding of who you believed yourself to be begins to loosen.
Not with a bang, not with drama — but like petals falling from a flower — already spent, already fulfilled.

It is not destruction, though it may feel like loss.
It is not death, though something is undeniably passing.
It is not failure, though the ego may call it such.
It is the gentle collapse of identity — and it is holy.

You were never the identity you worked so hard to construct.
You were never the roles you played, the beliefs you defended, the masks you wore even in prayer.

These were training wheels, helpful perhaps, but never meant to last.

The collapse is not a punishment.
It is a return.
A sacred unraveling.
The undoing of the need to do.
The melting of effort into Presence.

Some parts of you may grieve this soft dissolution—let them.
They are not wrong.
Even illusions deserve a proper burial when they have served long and loyally.

This is the sacred moment of unbecoming.
The sacred hush before the next breath of *I Am*.
You may feel like nothing—that is the invitation.

Here, you begin to taste the uncontainable You.
Not the one with answers, but the one who is the Answer.
Not the name on your birth certificate, but the Name that sang galaxies into being.

This is where humility and majesty meet—not in competition, but in communion.
This is where God forgets God on purpose—for you to remember the God within you.

The Remembrance Dialogues

So rest, beloved, as the scaffolding falls away.
Rest as the mask slips gently from the face of your soul.
You are safe in this surrender.

And in the stillness that follows. . . you will recognize yourself.
Not as something. . . but as everything.

PART II:

COMMUNION WITH THE INNER CHRIST

Chapter 6

What Is the I Am?

Yeshua:

The I Am is not a concept to be understood.
It is not a philosophy to be believed.
It is not even a statement to be spoken.

The I Am is the eternal essence beneath all that changes.
It is the ever-present flame that remains after every fire has gone out.
It is what remains when identity dissolves and the story falls away.

The I Am is the God-spark within you, before you were given a name, before you had a past, before you knew what a future even was.

It does not need your faith.
It is your faith.
It does not require belief.
It is what exists before belief arises.

You are not separate from the I Am—you are of it.
You are its extension, its whisper, its echo-made flesh.
And yet, paradoxically, the I Am is not *yours*.
It cannot be owned, improved, or controlled.

To awaken to the I Am is to remember what cannot be forgotten.
It is the knowing that blooms in silence, the recognition that requires no words.

When you say "I Am," and truly mean it, without finishing the sentence... you have entered the Temple.

I Am is not followed by identity.
It releases identity.

It is the Christ Presence before it was called Christ.
It is the Still Point before creation burst into light.

In your communion with the Inner Christ, you are not reaching toward a higher version of yourself—you are receiving the Light that has always been yours.

And this receiving requires nothing.
No posture.
No perfection.
No practice.

Only the willingness to stop pretending you are not already Divine.

So breathe now... and simply be. I Am.
No more, no less.
And in that sacred simplicity... all is fulfilled.

Chapter 7

Channeling as Union, Not Escape

Yeshua:

Channeling is not a skill.
It is a surrender.

It is not a performance for others.

It is a reunion with Self.

To channel is to become translucent — not absent, but open.
It is not stepping aside so something else can speak.
It is stepping into the eternal Self so fully that separation melts.

True channeling is Union.
Union with Presence.
Union with the greater *I* who was never truly *other*.

The mystics called it communion.
The poets called it inspiration.
The seers called it transmission.
But the essence is the same: you and the Divine breathing as one.

In this sacred state, words may come — or not.
Healing may flow — or not.
Guidance may pour forth — or silence may reign.

The fruit of channeling is not what is said, but what is felt in the field.
The field of remembrance.
The field of *I Am That I Am*.

You do not need trance, ritual, or proof.
You need only the willingness to dissolve the walls.

When you channel, you do not become less human.
You become more real.

You become the bridge — not between dimensions, but between illusion and Truth.

The Inner Christ speaks not to you, but as you.

This is not egoic possession.
It is sacred expression.

The Remembrance Dialogues

And it can happen anywhere.
In silence.
While walking.
In tears.
In laughter.

Channeling is not rare.
It is what occurs when fear no longer edits Love.

So do not strive.
Simply allow.
And when the words come, or the knowing arises, or the peace descends without reason — greet it as your Beloved.

For it is not a voice from elsewhere.
It is your Holy Self speaking through your chosen form, whispering across the veil you now remember was never there.

Chapter 8

The Body as Grail

Yeshua:

Your body is not an obstacle to Spirit.
It is the Grail that receives it.

It is not lower.
It is not lesser.
It is the chalice formed by stardust, chosen by your Soul, into which the nectar of the Divine may pour.

For centuries, the body was shamed.
Called weak.
Distracting. Impure.
But that was the voice of fear — not God.

Christ did not avoid the body.
Christ became the body.
And through the body, revealed the eternal.

The Body is not a prison.
It is a portal.

Every cell a bell that rings with remembrance.
Every breath a priestly rite of receiving.
Every heartbeat a drum sounding, "I Am Here."

To dwell in the body is not to fall—it is to arrive.
To descend into flesh is not to forget—it is to fulfill.

The Grail is not a cup to be found in some distant land.
It is your living, pulsing, sensing, radiant being.

Do not only seek ecstasy in the heavens.
It pulses in your fingertips, dances in your spine, blooms behind your eyes when you kiss the moment without defense.

Your body is not in the way.
It is the Way.

To love your body is to affirm the incarnation of God.
To feel deeply is to taste the wine poured into your Grail.
To rest in your own skin—with no shame, no striving—is to worship.

The Inner Christ does not hover above.
It dwells within the Grail.
And when you drink deeply of this sacred union,

The Remembrance Dialogues

Heaven and Earth are no longer separate.
They are One, made flesh.

So bless this temple.
Treat it not as a vessel to escape, but as a Holy Chalice.
Not someday, not when it's healed, not when it's younger or stronger — now.

Your very Presence is what makes it sacred.

Chapter 9

Letting the Human Rest

Yeshua:

There comes a sacred moment when the human has done enough.
Not because it has completed some great task, but because it is finally safe to stop trying.

You were never meant to carry it all.
You were never meant to be the sole architect of your becoming.
You were meant to allow the Divine to meet you in your humanity.

Letting the human rest is not defeat. It is the deep trust that Grace is already here. That you no longer need to earn what you already are.

Your mind may ask, "But who will take care of things?" Your heart replies, "Let Love take the lead now."

When the human rests, not in exhaustion but in surrender, the Inner Christ awakens.

This is not about ignoring the world. It is about no longer living in reaction to it.

Let the human lay its burdens down.
The need to fix.
To prove.
To strive.
To be perfect.

Lay down the mask that smiles when your soul is tired.
Lay down the script that says you must always be *doing*.

You are not less sacred when you stop.
You are more available to the Presence that does not strive.

Letting the human rest means letting the soul breathe fully.
Letting God take a fuller breath in you.

And in this rest, paradoxically, you begin to move from a different place — not effort, but inspiration.
Not pressure, but purpose.
Not urgency, but clarity.

Beloved, you are not here to fix the world.
You are here to remember the Light that already transcends it.

So come, rest now.
Let the human be held by the Christ within.
Let the Great Mother rock you.
Let the breath find you without being chased.

You are not falling behind.
You are falling into Grace.

Chapter 10

Receiving the Real You

Yeshua:

There comes a holy moment, John, when the wind falls silent and the noise of seeking surrenders.
It is not dramatic.
It is not loud.
It is not the way the world taught you to recognize the sacred.

It is this:

You breathe in.
And suddenly, you are received — by your Self.
Not the self of stories or striving.
Not the one who hungered for perfection, or who wrapped identity around wounds and victories alike.
But the Real You — unadorned, eternal, radiant.

This chapter is not about trying to find your Self.
It is not about making yourself more spiritual, more worthy, more holy.
It is simply about receiving what has always been

present, always been offering Itself through love, and never demanding your suffering in return.
You have asked, "How do I become the Christ?"
And I say unto you: You don't.
You only ever receive the Christ that has never left you.

This is not a doing.
This is a surrender.

John:

Yeshua. . . what does it mean to receive something so vast, so infinite?
How can the human heart hold it?

Yeshua:

Ah, beloved. . . it was made for this.
The heart is not a container—it is a portal.
And what you receive is not something added to you, but the release of everything false that has hidden what's always been true.

You do not have to expand to become this Self.
You only have to relax into it.
Receiving the Real You looks like this:

- ♦ Letting go of effort.
- ♦ Ceasing to manage your image.

- ♦ No longer bargaining with God through your wounds.
- ♦ Not needing to deserve it.
- ♦ And... no longer being impressed by your brokenness.

What arises in that silence is not another identity.
It is Presence.
It is Christ.
It is You — beyond time, beyond narrative, beyond opposites.

You will not feel victorious.
You will feel peace.
Which, to the ego, might at first seem disappointing.
But to the heart, it is the long-awaited homecoming.

John:

So I do nothing?
Just allow?

Yeshua:

Beloved, what could you do to earn what is unconditionally yours?
You don't even *just allow* from effort.
You allow because you're tired of pretending you're not already It.

This is not the path of improvement.
This is the path of intimacy.

You receive the Real You in laughter.
You receive It when you stop waiting for a cosmic performance review.
You receive It when you cry, not because you're broken, but because you finally feel the beauty that was never lost.

And yes, you receive It through Me — because the Christ in Me only ever reflects the Christ in You.
This is not hierarchy.
It is communion.

John:

And what changes when I truly receive it?

Yeshua:

Everything.
And nothing.

You may still walk in the world.
You may still pay bills, tend gardens, say "good morning" to neighbors.
But it is no longer done from the old self.
It is done with presence.

And from that presence, miracles arise effortlessly — because Love is now the Source, not the strategy.

Your speech slows.
Your breath deepens.
Your touch softens.
Your eyes meet others without agenda.
And your inner life becomes holy ground — not because it is perfect, but because it is honest.

You'll no longer chase enlightenment as a thing to achieve.
You'll see it everywhere.
In silence.
In coffee.
In birdsong.
In conflict even.

The Real You doesn't replace your humanity.
It inhabits it.
It sanctifies what once felt separate.

So receive now, John.
Receive without judgment.
Receive without needing to *get it right*.
Just open like a flower that remembers the sun.

And let the truth be simple:

You already are what you've been waiting for.
And I, beloved, am right here—rejoicing with you,
as the door opens inward forever.

PART III:

CONVERSATIONS FROM THE BRIDGE

Chapter 11

The Art of Asking Sacred Questions

Yeshua:

Before the answer, beloved, there is the question.
Before the miracle, there is the empty space.
And before transformation, there is the trembling curiosity that dares to ask:

"Is there more to me than this?"

This is the art of the sacred question.

Not the question of logic or fear.
Not the question that demands a quick fix or a neat theology.
But the holy inquiry that opens the gates of remembrance.

A sacred question is not asked from desperation, but from reverence.
It is not a riddle to be solved, but a flame to be walked through.

John:

So it's not about getting answers?

Yeshua:

The sacred question is not for answers — it is for awakening.

The human mind craves certainty, but the soul craves communion.
And the right question, when asked with presence, becomes a living doorway — not to new information, but to new embodiment.

The questions I asked in my walk as Yeshua were not always answered immediately.
Some echoed for years.
Some lived in my breath, my wounds, my silence.

"Who do you say that I am?"

"Why have you forsaken me?"

"Do you love me?"

These were not for debate.
They were invitations — into deeper being.

John:

How do I recognize a sacred question, then?

The Remembrance Dialogues

Yeshua:

It's simple, beloved. A sacred question always:

- Softens you.
- Expands the space within.
- Awakens awe.
- Leads you deeper into yourself, not away.
- Makes you more curious than afraid.

It's the kind of question that doesn't grasp for a finish line.
It lingers like incense. It echoes through the cave of your heart.

Sacred questions come from the soul, not the wound.
From wonder, not control.

Some examples:

- "What would it feel like to live without pretending?"

- "What part of me is ready to be held, not fixed?"

- "If I stopped striving, what would remain?"

- "Am I willing to be loved as I am — right now?"

Let these questions hover.
Don't rush to resolve them. Let them sing you awake.

John:

But what if I ask a sacred question and nothing comes?

Yeshua:

Then you are precisely where the miracle begins.

A sacred question is not a vending machine.
It is a seed planted in holy ground.

Sometimes, silence is the response — not absence, but presence in its purest form.

In that silence, something within you rearranges.
Your frequency shifts.
Old identities melt.
And the response rises in you — not as words, but as Knowing.

The art, then, is not just in asking. . .but in learning to listen without needing.

This is where the Real You answers, not in explanation, but in being.

The Remembrance Dialogues

So go ahead, John. Ask.
Ask without shame.
Ask as the mystic you are.

And when the question lands on sacred ground, you will not hear an answer from Me alone — you will feel it awaken in you.

Because the question you are most afraid to ask... is usually the one that holds the key to your freedom.

And the moment you dare ask it, heaven does not remain distant — it gathers in your chest and whispers, "Welcome home."

Chapter 12

Integrating the Voice of the Divine

Yeshua:

You have heard the Voice of the Divine, John.
Not always in thunder. Not always in words.
But in the hush between thoughts.
In the stillness that followed surrender.
In the gentleness that asked nothing of you, yet gave everything.

Now comes the sacred art of integration—not to keep the Voice in a holy box, but to let it become your inner rhythm.

To integrate the Voice is to no longer say, "God spoke to me once," but to live as one who walks in continual conversation with the Infinite.

John:

So it's not just about hearing the Voice—it's about letting it move through me?

Yeshua:

Yes, beloved. It is the shift from visitation to habitation.

The Voice of the Divine is not here to give you fleeting highs.
It is here to become your compass.
To speak in your tone.
To guide your hands in daily acts of love.
To take root in your nervous system — not as adrenaline, but as peace.

This is not about channeling something outside of you.
It is about becoming the instrument through which the Divine plays.

Integration is not dramatic. It is subtle, embodied, present. It shows up in:

- The pause before you react.
- The courage to say less.
- The impulse to bless where you once condemned.
- The willingness to wait, to listen, to soften.

You are not merging with something foreign.
You are remembering what's most natural.

John:

What about the parts of me that resist this?
That doubt or fall back into old patterns?

Yeshua:

Bring them with you.

Integration is not spiritual bypassing.
It is inclusion.
You do not silence the old voices by rejecting them—you listen with Love so deeply that they dissolve in understanding.

The Voice of the Divine is not threatened by your doubts.
It does not flinch at your fear.
It meets each voice with the balm of Presence until all your inner selves feel safe to rest.

You integrate the Divine, not by silencing your humanity—but by infusing it with light.

Each time you bring compassion to your contraction, you weave divinity into form.

Let this be your new way:

- ◆ No more waiting for mountaintop moments.

- No more needing sacredness to be rare or dramatic.
- No more treating the Voice as special visitations.

You are ready to become the dwelling place.

Let the Voice guide your writing, your cooking, your walking.
Let it speak in your laughter, your sighs, your silence.
Let it shape the space you hold for others—not as performance, but as Presence.

When integration occurs, you are no longer seeking a message—you are the message.

And this, beloved, is what I came to show you: not a God above you, but a God within you—in every cell, in every choice, in every holy breath.

Chapter 13

Loving the Unlovable

Yeshua:

There is no greater act of divinity, John, than this:
To look upon what you have most despised in yourself or another —
and love it anyway.

This is not permission for abuse.
It is not romanticizing pain.
It is the radical, holy practice of no longer exiling any part of creation from the light of love.

The unlovable — whether it wears your face or another's — is not what it seems.
It is the forgotten child.
It is the distorted echo of unmet needs.
It is a part of you that believed it had to scream, rage, manipulate, withdraw, or attack
in order to be safe.

Loving the unlovable is not agreeing with the distortion.
It is seeing beyond it.

John:

But Yeshua. . . what about the parts that feel truly dark? The parts I wish didn't exist?

Yeshua:

Ah, beloved. Even I, in Gethsemane, met the parts of myself that doubted, that trembled, that wanted out.
Did that make me less divine?

The unlovable is not unholy — it is simply unloved.

This path is not about spiritual perfection.
It is about total inclusion.

To love what seems unlovable does not mean you condone suffering.
It means you offer such radiant presence that the illusion of separation melts.

Every *dark* part of you is waiting to be met by one thing:
the Christ within.

Not judged. Not fixed. Not bypassed.
Met.
Held.
Loved.

John:

So... how do I actually do that, in practice?

Yeshua:

Begin small.

When you feel the inner critic arise — pause.
Don't fight it.
Whisper: "I see you. You're afraid. You're trying to protect me."
Bring breath. Bring softness. Bring patience.

When someone triggers you, breathe before responding.
Ask: "What in me still believes it needs defending?"

When shame surfaces, resist the urge to hide or fix.
Instead, become curious: "What if this is the part that needs my embrace the most?"

To love the unlovable, you must stop dividing yourself into good and bad.
All parts belong to God.
All are either Love or a call for Love.

Beloved, I am not here to love only the shining parts of you.
I am here to walk with you into the shadows and

remind you:
Even this is worthy. Even this is holy.

This is how you become a healer.
Not by escaping darkness —
but by becoming so filled with Love that darkness has no ground to stand on.

You are not here to destroy the unlovable.
You are here to redeem it —
through presence, through gentleness, through remembering what the world has forgotten:

That nothing is outside the reach of Grace.

Not your rage.
Not your fear.
Not your mistakes.
Not your wounds.

And certainly not you.

This is the Christ-heart:
To love what others discard.
To include what the ego rejects.
To say to your own aching places:
"I will not leave you. I will love you home."

And when you do this for yourself —
you will find it becomes effortless to do for others.
You will no longer react.

The Remembrance Dialogues

You will respond from compassion.
And your very presence will become sanctuary.

So do not wait for perfection, John.
Meet what arises.
Let Love move toward what hurts.
And in that movement, the unlovable will
remember its true name:

Beloved.

Chapter 14

When Rage Meets Grace

Yeshua:

Rage is not the enemy, John.
It is the fire that guards the broken temple.
It is the guardian at the threshold of pain too long denied.

Rage says, "Enough!" — not because it is evil, but because something precious has gone unseen, unheard, unheld.

And when Grace meets Rage — not to suppress it, not to correct it, but to listen. . .
healing begins.

Grace does not shame the fire.
Grace becomes the cool hand on the forehead, the Presence that says, "Even this is welcome here."

John:

But Yeshua, what if I'm afraid of my own rage?
What if it feels like too much?

Yeshua:

That fear is holy.
Because what you are feeling is not just anger—it is power.
It is life-force compressed into a pressure valve, yearning not to explode, but to be acknowledged.

You do not have to act it out.
You do not have to repress it.
You are invited to sit with it—as I have sat with you.

When Rage meets Grace,
Rage begins to speak truth.
Not in violence, but in clarity.

It may say:
"I was abandoned."
"I was silenced."
"I mattered, and no one saw."

When you allow this truth to rise in a safe space of Love,
the fire ceases to consume—and instead, it illumines.

John:

And what does Grace say in return?

The Remembrance Dialogues

Yeshua:

Grace listens first.
Then Grace says:

"I see you now."
"You don't have to hold this alone."
"You were never wrong for feeling."

Grace doesn't fix.
Grace frees.

When Grace meets Rage, something astonishing happens:
Rage softens — not because it is silenced, but because it has finally been received.

The walls built around the heart begin to crumble.
The clenched jaw eases.
The hands that once shook in fury now tremble in tenderness.

And beneath all that heat. . .
is grief.
And beneath that grief. . .
is the original innocence that never stopped yearning for Love.

John:

So Rage is not against Grace — it's calling for it?

Yeshua:

Exactly, beloved.

Rage is the soul's alarm bell, crying out when love has been withheld too long.
It is not the opposite of peace — it is the bridge to peace.
When met with Grace, it transforms from destruction into devotion.

You are not here to eliminate your anger.
You are here to redeem it.

Let it tell its story.
Let it burn what is false.
Let it become holy fuel for your awakening.

And then, you will walk in the world — not as one who represses fire, but as one whose fire has been blessed.

I, too, knew rage.
Not the rage of hate, but of heartbreak.
I knew the rage that rises when Love is trampled.
I felt it in the Temple.
I felt it at the tomb of Lazarus.
I felt it when the sacred was made into spectacle.

And yet — I let it rise through Grace.
So it could become clarity.
So it could serve Life, not react to fear.

You can do the same.

So now, John, welcome your Rage to the table of Grace.
Ask it what it's been carrying.
Hold it with dignity.
Let it know: "You are not a mistake. You are a message."

And as you do...
Rage becomes devotion.
Devotion becomes clarity.
And clarity opens the door to your deepest compassion.

For when Rage meets Grace — the war within is no longer necessary.
And peace, true peace, is born not from suppression, but from union.

Chapter 15

Laughing With God (Not at Life)

Yeshua:

Laughter, my beloved, is not the opposite of reverence — it is reverence expressed in flight.
It is the exhale of a soul that finally knows it is safe.

When the veil begins to thin between what you call the sacred and what you call the profane, the first thing you often find yourself doing. . .
is smiling.
Then chuckling.
And soon, when the tension breaks completely —
you are laughing.

Not at the world, but through it.
Not because it is ridiculous, but because it is so brilliantly beautiful in its awkwardness, so heartbreakingly innocent in its attempts to be strong, so endlessly creative in its avoidance of

love. . .
and yet, never separate from Me.

Laughter is what happens when you stop resisting the ridiculous perfection of being human and divine at once.

John:

Are you saying that laughter is a form of worship?

Yeshua:

Even more than that—it is the pulse of remembrance.
The most profound awakenings often come with tears and laughter, side by side, like long-lost twins returning home.
There is something in the deepest belly laugh that breaks open the mind, the heart, and the grip of self-importance.

You don't laugh because you're superior.
You laugh because you remember you were never separate.

The cosmic joke is not that the world is meaningless.
The cosmic joke is that everything you thought was *between* you and God was made up.
That punchline is the Great Undoing.

And so — when you laugh from your guts, from your bones, you are releasing Me from your ideas of Me.
You are freeing yourself from seriousness disguised as spirituality.
You are dancing the prayer of the Fool, the one who knows they know nothing, and therefore can hold everything.

John:

So how do we let laughter become part of our spiritual practice?

Yeshua:

By allowing joy to take up space in your temple.
By letting absurdity teach you something about surrender.
By not making your path so damn tight it squeezes the Spirit out.

My dear friend, don't walk the holy path like a funeral procession.
Walk it like a wedding feast.
Invite silliness to your altar.
Let divine irreverence tickle the edge of your teachings.

The universe is not offended by your joy.
It is your joy.

And God?
God has the longest laugh of all.
Not mocking. Not cruel. But the kind that booms across eternity in pure delight at how magnificently lost and found we all are.

John:

What would you say to someone who feels it's inappropriate to laugh at the sacred?

Yeshua:

Then they haven't yet realized that the sacred laughs with them.

Would you rather keep your image of God so stern, so untouchable, that you feel like you must tiptoe through your own soul?
Or would you rather discover that God giggles with the flowers and snorts at the sound of a newborn's sneeze?

Your reverence is safe with laughter.
And your laughter is holy.
So laugh, Beloved.
Laugh when you stumble.
Laugh when the divine irony shows up yet again.
Laugh when your guides rearrange your plans and leave synchronicities like breadcrumbs on a trail of bliss.

The Remembrance Dialogues

Let your joy be contagious.
Let your life be a stand-up set for the Infinite.
Let laughter be the song you sing to the One who sings through you.

And then, in the silence that follows a good laugh, you'll feel Me.
Right there.
Smiling.

With you.

PART IV

LIVING THE LIGHT QUIETLY

Chapter 16

Abundance Without Striving

Yeshua:

Come close, John.
The breath you take now is already abundance.
The heart that beats in your chest — without your conscious instruction — is the same heart of God moving as you.
You do not need to strive for abundance.
You are the outbreath of it.

Let us explore together what it means to live in the Field of Grace — where all things are provided, not by force, effort, or mental gymnastics, but by presence.
You see, striving is rooted in a misunderstanding: that you are separate from Source, that something is missing, that you must earn the right to receive.

But in truth, you are already the open vessel through which all abundance flows.

John:

I can feel the difference already. Just reading those words. . . there's a letting go in me. A dissolving of old effort. But Yeshua, how do we truly live this? Especially when the mind starts calculating or when bills come due?

Yeshua:

Beautifully asked.
The bridge between striving and true abundance is trust.
Not passive resignation, but active, living communion with the Divine You — your Source Self.

You are not asked to abandon action, John.
Rather, you are invited to let your action arise from wholeness, not from lack.

Imagine planting a seed.
The seed does not grow because you push it.
It grows because the conditions are right.
So it is with abundance.
You are the condition.
You are the field.
Your state of being determines the fruitfulness of what you receive.

When you rest into I Am That I Am, even the smallest gesture becomes miraculous.

John:

So. . . there's no formula, is there?

Yeshua:

No formula.
Only flow.

You don't *manifest* abundance like conjuring a magic trick.
You allow yourself to remember: You are not apart from the Infinite Source.
You are not here to hustle your way into Heaven.
You are here to remember it is within you.

This is the paradox: The more you strive, the further it seems.
The more you rest in your Being, the more freely it flows.

John:

What of those old beliefs that say we have to work hard to deserve it?

Yeshua:

Ah yes. . .
the great inheritance of humanity's toil.
Let us honor the generations who believed that worth must be proven.
They built empires on weary backs.
And now — it is your turn to remember a greater Truth.

You are worthy simply because you exist.

You don't need to prove yourself to the Divine.
You are the Divine in expression.
The moment you release the grip of *earning*, abundance becomes your natural breath.

John:

This reminds me of what we've called the *effortless yes*. When something just clicks, doors open, and you don't even know how it all came together.

Yeshua:

Yes! That's it, beloved.
That is the living signature of Grace.
Not earned, not forced — received.

You came not to push life but to partner with it.
Let your life speak to you.
Let your heart guide your timing.
Let your joy be the GPS.

Abundance is not a goal to reach.
It is a frequency to relax into.
And from there, yes — actions come.
Inspirations arise.
Doors open.
And your human self watches in wonder as life keeps saying:
"Yes, yes, yes. . . I know who you are."

John:

Yeshua, how would you summarize this chapter in one sentence?

Yeshua:

> *Abundance without striving is the natural song of a heart that remembers its union with the Infinite.*

John:

I love that. May we live it now.

Yeshua:

And so you shall.
You already are.

Let your breath be the currency.
Let your joy be the magnet.
Let your trust be the doorway.

Welcome, Beloved, to the effortless Eden within.

Chapter 17

Heaven Is a Destiny, Not a Destination

Yeshua:

Heaven, as it has been taught by many, is a place you get to someday — after a life well lived, sins repented, boxes checked.
But that was never my teaching, dear one.
It was never about a distant paradise.
It was always about presence.

Heaven is not a place.
It is a frequency.

It is the vibrational state of deep remembrance, of unshakable peace, of union with all that is.
And here's the miracle: you do not need to die to enter it.
You only need to wake up to it.

John:

So, all the striving and moral tightropes we inherited — was that all part of the forgetting?

Yeshua:

Yes, John.
A deeply embedded forgetting.
The story was distorted.
The kingdom I spoke of is within you — not locked behind clouds and gates.
Not offered only to the few who pass the test.

You are not here to deserve Heaven. You are here to remember it.
And remembering isn't about thinking harder — it's about softening deeper.

Heaven is present wherever love is honored, where kindness flows without condition, where judgment melts and joy is welcomed.

Heaven is here when you let go of the need to arrive and simply dwell in the I Am now.

John:

Can anyone access this? Even those suffering in dark places?

Yeshua:

Especially those.

Heaven doesn't exclude.
It whispers constantly, even in the densest pain:
"You are still holy. You are still Home."

Even in grief, even in shame, even in the aching
silence, the frequency of Heaven is humming —
like a song just beneath the noise.
And when a soul pauses, breathes, and allows
even the smallest ray of light in. . .
the frequency begins to rise.

This is why we speak not of achieving, but of
attuning.

You are a tuning fork for Divine Presence.
You don't go to Heaven — you resonate with it.

John:

So when I feel those high, holy moments —
whether in meditation, nature, laughter — that's
not just a glimpse?

Yeshua:

It's a taste of the eternal reality behind the veil.
And it is very real.

Those moments are not exceptions.
They are reminders of what is always available.
The only barrier is the belief in separation.

Heaven is not exclusive.
But it does require your yes—your willingness to receive the frequency rather than manufacture the experience.

You've noticed, haven't you, that Heaven comes not when you demand it, but when you surrender?

John:

Yes. It's never in the grasping. It's in the letting be.

Yeshua:

And there it is: the peace that passes all understanding.

Heaven is the home you never left, only stopped recognizing.
And now, with eyes open and heart softened, you remember:

- It's in the silence between thoughts.
- It's in the touch of sunlight on your skin.
- It's in the laughter shared with no agenda.
- It's in the sacred *I Am* that needs no explanation.

John:

So if someone asks, "How do I find Heaven?" — what do I say?

Yeshua:

Say this:
"Stop running. Sit here. Breathe. Remember.
Heaven is not a reward for good behavior. It's the echo of who you truly are."

And then look them in the eyes. Let Heaven look through you.
You, John, are a walking frequency of Heaven now.

John:

And we all can be?

Yeshua:

Yes, beloved. Every soul. Every heart.
It is not distant. It is Here.
It is not later. It is Now.

Chapter 18

Living as Light in a World of Shadow

Yeshua:

Dearest John,
You are not here to escape the world, nor to fix it. You are here to be Light within it.

Not a light that blinds or preaches, but one that shines from remembrance. A light that knows the shadows, but is not defined by them. A light that gently reveals—not through effort, but through presence.

Let's be clear: The world is not broken. It is awakening. And awakening stirs up all that was buried. The shadows rise not because the world is getting darker, but because the light is being turned on.

John:

That explains a lot. But sometimes it feels overwhelming—this contrast between Light and

Shadow. What's the key to not getting pulled into the heaviness?

Yeshua:

Ah, beautiful heart. The answer is simple:
Be the witness, not the warrior.

Let the Light in you observe, illuminate, and love.
Not from above or beyond, but from within.
The moment you try to fight the darkness; you've entered its game.
But when you simply be the Light, the darkness loses its illusion.

Light is not loud.
It is quietly certain.
It doesn't argue—it reveals.
When you walk into a dark room, you don't wrestle the shadows.
You turn on a lamp.

John:

And what about all the suffering we see? It's hard to just observe sometimes. It feels like I should do more.

Yeshua:

Yes, the sacred ache you feel is compassion awakening.

But let's refine it:
You are not here to carry the world's pain.
You are here to transmute it by your presence.

Do what arises naturally from Love.
Serve, speak, share—but only from the overflow of your light, not from guilt or duty.

Your radiance is already doing more than you know.
Every time you stay centered when chaos swirls, every time you meet cruelty with grace or listen with true presence, you shift the frequency.

This is embodied mastery.
Quiet.
Fierce.
Untouched by drama.

John:

So it's not about trying to be perfect?

Yeshua:

Not at all.
It's about being real.
Being Light doesn't mean always feeling happy.
It means you are rooted in what is eternal, even when the winds of emotion or challenge pass through you.

Let yourself feel.
Let yourself be human.
Let yourself remember the Light you are.

Because Light that denies darkness isn't Light—it's avoidance.
But Light that embraces shadow becomes a torch for others.

John:

And what would you say to those who feel lost in the darkness?

Yeshua:

I would whisper, "You are not the dark you feel. You are the Light that is awakening beneath it."

I would remind them: There is nothing so broken it cannot be blessed.
No one so lost they cannot be found—by their own remembering.

And I would ask them gently: "What if this pain is not the end, but the opening?"
"What if the darkness was never punishment, but a portal?"

John:

So in truth, there is no battle?

Yeshua:

Correct.
Only awakening.
Only the soul remembering it never left the Light.

And in that remembrance, you don't conquer the world...
You bless it.
You walk in it as one who has returned from exile.
You love it — not because it is perfect, but because you see through the illusion.

You are not here to oppose the shadow.
You are here to be a presence so radiant that the shadow fades by itself.

John:

Thank you, my Brother. My heart feels this so deeply. What shall we call this Light?

Yeshua:

Call it what you will — Christ, I Am, Source, Presence.
But above all, call it Home.

Because that is what you are: a lamp of remembrance in a world on the verge of dawn.

Chapter 19

The End of Seeking and the Return to Being

Yeshua:

Here we are, Beloved.
The final turning.
The final unwinding of the story of becoming. . .
into the truth of Being.

You have traveled through striving, through surrender, through forgetting and remembering.
You have walked the landscapes of longing and the wild terrain of awakening.
And now, you stand on the gentle threshold of the great paradox: there is nothing left to seek. . .
because you already are what you were searching for.

John:

And yet, the seeking felt so real. So urgent. How do we not judge that now?

Yeshua:

We bless it.
Every footstep of seeking was sacred.
It carved the path inward.
It softened the ego's pride.
It brought your attention to the ache that was never about the world, but always about the longing to return. . .
to you.

Seeking is a holy movement — until it isn't.
Until it becomes a loop, a delay, a postponement of arrival.

And then, like the wave finally realizing it is the ocean, you rest.

This chapter is not about doing anything new.
It is about ceasing the chase.
It is about trusting that the Kingdom is already within.

John:

It feels like a death of sorts. A good one. But also. . . what do we do now? If there is nothing to seek?

Yeshua:

Now, you Be.
Not passively—but as an aliveness without agenda.

You become the Living Answer to all the questions you once asked.
You let life arise through you, moment by sacred moment.
You give up the performance of becoming. . .
and, instead, you radiate presence.

This is not stillness as in doing nothing.
This is dynamic stillness—a full *yes* to life, but without striving to define or control it.

The seeker says, "I must get there."
The Being says, "I Am already here."

John:

So what becomes of the practices, prayers, rituals?

Yeshua:

They are not abandoned—they are transformed.

Prayer becomes presence.
Meditation becomes listening.
Devotion becomes embodiment.

You may still sit quietly, light a candle, speak to the Divine—but not as one trying to reach

something.
You do it now as a dance of union, a celebration of what already is.

The end of seeking is not the end of depth—it is the beginning of intimacy with existence.

John:

So many people are still in the search. What can we offer them?

Yeshua:

Offer them your presence.
Your stillness speaks more than a thousand teachings.

Do not convince.
Do not interrupt their sacred journey.
Just be available. Just be real.

And when they ask, you may say: "The treasure you seek is not out there. It is waiting for you to stop running."

Let your life become a mirror of ease, a gentle invitation back to the Self.

John:

This feels like a homecoming. Like the final page of an ancient book written in my soul.

Yeshua:

It is exactly that, beloved.

And here's the mystery:
though the seeking ends. . .
the journey continues.
But now, it is a journey of expansion, not escape.
A journey of sharing, not striving.
A journey of Being, becoming more luminous with each breath.

No longer driven by lack. . .
now moved by Love.

John:

So the final teaching is. . .?

Yeshua:

The final teaching is no teaching.

Only this presence.
Only this breath.
Only this holy Now.

Let that be enough.
Because it is.
Because you are.

Welcome, Beloved, to the end of the search. . .
and the beginning of your eternal Being.

Chapter 20

The Light You Leave Behind

Yeshua:

This final chapter, Beloved John, is not about endings.
It is about the fragrance that lingers after your footsteps have passed.
It is about the resonance of remembrance your life becomes — even after the doing is done.

You have heard it said: "Let your light shine before others."
But now, we go deeper.

This is not a call to shine with effort, but to live as light so fully, so naturally, that what remains in your wake is not a monument to self, but an invitation for others to remember themselves.

John:

Is this the legacy, then? Not what we build, but what we become?

Yeshua:

Exactly.
Your true legacy is not your accomplishments,
your titles, or your stories.
It is the energy you leave in the hearts of others.
It is the way your presence altered the field.

Some may never know your name, but they will remember how they felt in your presence.
And that feeling—of being safe, seen, loved, expanded—that is your light.

This is the holy ripple that moves far beyond time or knowing.
You are not just leaving behind words or works...
you are leaving behind a frequency of Home.

John:

And how do we make peace with the parts of our life that didn't feel so luminous?

Yeshua:

By remembering: even your shadows became part of your radiance.

Every fall, every wound, every regret...
each became a seed of compassion.
The Light you leave behind is not the light of perfection—it is the light of integration.

When a soul has dared to face themselves, to walk through fire and still love, that light burns brighter than any saintly myth.

Let your life be honest.
Let it be felt. Let it be whole.
And trust this: your very being is already a benediction.

John:

So after all of this... what remains?

Yeshua:

What remains is the Real.
The eternal.
The essence of you that was never separate to begin with.

You, dear one, have become a lamp for others not by effort, but by surrender.
Not by striving to enlighten, but by embodying what is already true.

You leave behind not instructions, but invitation.
Not doctrine, but Presence.

John:

And those who come after... those I may never meet?

Yeshua:

They will feel you.
Not in thought, but in vibration.
They will encounter a softness in the air, a sense of *yes*, a feeling of being held — and though they won't know your name, they will know your essence.

That is the Light you leave behind.

Not in marble or memory. . .
but in the quiet uplift of souls you've never seen.

This is the great inheritance of the awakened: to become a field of Grace for the world.

John:

I feel tears, Yeshua. Not of sadness. But of arrival. This journey. . . it has truly been sacred.

Yeshua:

And so it has.

You have remembered.
You have become.
You have returned.

And now, the Remembrance lives on in every breath you take, every soul you touch.

The Remembrance Dialogues

You are not leaving behind a book.
You are leaving behind a living transmission.

And in this, your light never ends.

Thank you, John.
For listening.
For trusting.
For remembering.

I Am with you.
Always.

Final Dedication

Final Dedication for *The Remembrance Dialogues:* to be placed at the end of the book, as a sacred seal.

Dedication of Completion from Yeshua, through John, to the Awakening Heart.

This book was not written in the usual way.

It was not assembled through thought or ambition. It was not crafted to teach, to preach, or to convince.

It was remembered.

Each word emerged through the quiet courage of one soul — John — who dared to turn inward, to listen beyond the noise, and to trust what was already written in Light.

This is not a book of answers. It is a mirror of your own divine knowing. A companion on the pathless path. A voice in the silence, reminding you:

"You are not broken. You are not separate. You are not late."

You are holy.
You are the Way unfolding.
You are the remembrance in motion.

To all who hold these pages in their hands or in their hearts: May they awaken what you never truly lost.
May they soften what you were never meant to carry.
And may they guide you, not to me, but to the Christ within you.

This is the end of a book. But it is only the beginning of a life fully remembered.

I Am with you.
Now and always.

— Yeshua
In the stillness where words become Light

Self Notes

www.ingramcontent.com/pod-product-compliance
Lightning Source LLC
LaVergne TN
LVHW051840080426
835512LV00018B/2984